ROUEN TRAVEL GUIDE 2023

Unveiling Rouen: Your Ultimate Guide to
Exploring Rouen's Rich Heritage, Historical
Landmark, Vibrant Culture, Local Cuisine,
Itinerary, and Day Trips for First Timers

Mark E. Fears

Table Of Contents

My Unforgettable Rouen Travel Experience

Traveling to Rouen was like entering a time capsule where the history books came to life against a backdrop of beautiful architecture, cultural diversity, and a sense of calm serenity. I couldn't help but feel as though I was walking in the footsteps of centuries of tales as I traveled through the cobblestone streets and admired the magnificent cathedrals, with each turn of the city revealing a fresh aspect of its alluring past.

When I arrived, the city's distinctive fusion of medieval and contemporary elements was the first thing that grabbed my eye. My attention was drawn to the delicate intricacies of the Rouen Cathedral's tall spires as they rose magnificently against the sky. The half-timbered houses in the historic district seemed to be stuck in time as I walked through it; each façade revealed the history of the generations that had come before. With its elaborate clock face, the Gros Horloge served as a quiet testament to the passage of time and the city's everlasting ties to the past.

I strolled along the banks of the Seine River, a silent observer of Rouen's development, which provided a tranquil backdrop. I could think about the history of the city while taking in the soft breeze and the calming sound of the water on the little waterfront promenades. This river, which was once a route for trade and discovery, now provided comfort and tranquillity for both locals and tourists.

A voyage into the core of artistic expression was had by visiting the museums and galleries in Rouen. A wide range of artworks from many eras and stylistic movements were on display at the Musée des Beaux-Arts. Every brushstroke and sculpture, whether they were modern works of art or historic masterpieces, appeared to capture the aesthetic spirit of the city. I connected with Claude Monet's inspiration as I stood in front of his masterpieces as if the city's landscapes had revealed their secrets to him.

It was a sensory experience in and of itself to indulge in Rouen's culinary treats. As I strolled through neighborhood markets, filled with stalls brimming with colorful vegetables and artisanal delicacies, the scent of freshly baked baguettes filled the air. My taste senses were first introduced to the culinary wonders of the area by the delicate flavors of Camembert cheese and the pleasing richness of an apple dessert made in the tradition of Normandy.

Whether it was stumbling across a secret courtyard decorated with blooming flowers or finding a charming café nestled away in a quiet alley, Rouen appeared to hold a surprise around every bend. My experience was enhanced and my travel took on a more personal touch as a result of my interactions with the kind locals who kindly offered their stories and recommendations.

I couldn't help but feel incredibly grateful for the chance to see Rouen's charm as the sun fell below the horizon, putting a warm glow on the city's medieval buildings. The history, culture, and natural beauty of the city had weaved themselves into my heart, leaving an enduring imprint that would bind me to this magical place forever.

Though leaving Rouen was difficult, I did so with a fresh understanding of the value of preserving history and valuing the beauty of the present. I carried with me the echoes of Rouen's past, the whispers of its legends, and the hope of its enduring charm. My vacation experience had been a tapestry of moments, feelings, and discoveries.

1. Introduction To Rouen

1.1 Overview of Rouen

Rouen is a French city located in the Normandy area that stands as a city rich in history, culture, and architectural splendor. It is tucked away along the serene banks of the Seine River. Rouen has earned its status as a jewel of the northwest of the country with its cobblestone streets, soaring churches, and a rich tapestry of stories woven into its fabric.

Since the Middle Ages, Rouen has been a prominent commerce center due to its advantageous position. The city's gorgeous location on the Seine River, which splits it into two halves connected by opulent bridges, adds to its allure. A harmonious fusion of nature and society is created by the surrounding terrain, which is made up of undulating hills and verdant farmland.

The architecture of the city provides evidence of its historical importance. The magnificent Gothic Rouen

Cathedral, which Claude Monet immortalized in his well-known "Rouen Cathedral Series," serves as a prime example of the city's architectural magnificence. With its elaborate design and usefulness, the Gros-Horloge, a magnificent astronomical clock from the 14th century, continues to enthrall tourists.

Every part of Rouen is infused with the rich cultural legacy of the city. The Joan of Arc Tower and Museum honors the illustrious French heroine who was infamously tried and executed in Rouen's market square. A sense of traveling back in time is evoked by the city's medieval streets, which are dotted with timber-framed homes. The Renaissance to the modern day is represented in the collection of artworks on display at the Musée des Beaux-Arts.

Rouen's history is intricately entwined with the history of France. When the Hundred Years War broke out, Normandy, which was once the Duchy of Normandy's capital, was there to witness Joan of Arc's trial and subsequent martyrdom. During the Middle Ages, the city's commercial prowess developed, promoting commerce and cross-cultural interaction. With its monasteries and institutions, it was also a significant center of scholarship and religion.

A delicious representation of Rouen's Norman past can be seen in its culinary scene. The famed Camembert and Livarot kinds are only two of the city's world-famous cheeses. In Rouen, dining options range from little cafes providing traditional Norman cuisine to sophisticated eateries serving creative takes on time-honored delicacies.

Rouen is a bustling urban city that is nonetheless steeped in history. The city is infused with modern vigor by the booming arts sector, exciting festivals, and bustling marketplaces. The Armada Festival, an annual maritime festival that attracts stunning tall ships to the riverbanks, is evidence of Rouen's longstanding maritime ties.

In essence, Rouen is a city that successfully combines its rich past with its vibrant current. Visitors are encouraged to wander its streets, learn about its culture, and experience time travel through its distinctive fusion of architecture, culture, and natural beauty. All who walk through Rouen's streets are left with an enduring impression of the city's alluring allure, which is cast with each stride.

1.2 Rouen's History

The fascinating story of conquest, aristocracy, and tenacity that makes up Rouen's history spans more than two thousand years. Rouen's history is a witness to its continuous relevance in the chronicles of France, from its early days as a Roman town to its crucial role during the Hundred Years' War.

Roman ancestry:
The Roman town of Rotomagus, founded in the first century AD, is where Rouen's origins can be found. The town prospered under Roman authority as an important hub for trade and commerce, gaining from its advantageous location along the Roman road networks.

Middle Age Ascendancy:

The rise of Rouen to prominence occurred during the Middle Ages. Under the leadership of the Viking chieftain Rollo, who converted to Christianity and founded a dynasty, the city was made the seat of the Duchy of Normandy in the ninth century. Under the rule of William the Conqueror, who began the Norman Conquest of England in 1066, the duchy's influence considerably increased.

The 100 Years' War:

During the Hundred Years' War (1337–1453), Rouen's history underwent a significant change. The city, which was the center of the English-French conflict, was subjected to numerous sieges and battles. The trial and execution of Joan of Arc in 1431, an act that would permanently associate her name with Rouen, was perhaps the most dramatic happening during this time.

Renaissance and Later:

Rouen experienced new riches during the Renaissance. The city's traders conducted profitable trade with the

New World, which boosted its economy. Architectural marvels, such as the well-known Rouen Cathedral, were built during this period, showing the city's vibrant creative and cultural life.

Modernity with the Industrial Revolution:
Rouen suffered change once the Industrial Revolution got underway. Its manufacturing and textile sectors prospered, further solidifying its position as an economic center. Despite the damage, Rouen was able to recover and preserve its historic center. Rouen could not, however, escape the problems of modernity, and it experienced catastrophe during World War II.

Artistic and Cultural Heritage:
Rouen has inspired writers and painters throughout its history. The play of light on the cathedral's façade was caught in Claude Monet's renowned "Rouen Cathedral Series" in various climatic conditions. Numerous poets, writers, and artists have been inspired by the city's attractive architecture and ancient streets.

Rouen's geography and climate:

The location of Rouen, which is tucked away in the French region of Normandy, is nothing short of magical. The city's strategic location along the Seine River has historically fostered trade and cross-cultural interchange. Gentle hills, lush valleys, and gorgeous farmlands make up the area's topography, which provides an alluring setting for Rouen's architectural beauty.

The Seine River connects Rouen to both Paris and the English Channel, acting as a lifeline for the city. The development of the city has benefited greatly from this river, which also promotes trade and shapes the local identity. The arrangement of the city has developed around the river, creating quaint waterfronts, active docks, and picturesque promenades that attract locals and guests to take in the beauty of the area.

The proximity of Rouen to the coast has an impact on its climate, resulting in a moderate maritime environment with warm summers and somewhat mild winters. The

Seine River's presence further regulates temperature, resulting in a comfortable environment all year long. Winter temperatures range from 2°C to 6°C (36°F to 43°F), while acceptable summer temperatures range from 18°C to 25°C (64°F to 77°F). The year-round even distribution of rainfall contributes to the region's luxuriant flora.

1.3 Things to Know Before Travelling to Rouen

To guarantee a smooth and rewarding trip to Rouen, there are a few important considerations to bear in mind before leaving:

**1. Accept the Past: Rouen's history is entwined with important occasions, including the Viking invasions and Joan of Arc's trial. For a deeper understanding of the significance of the city's landmarks and cultural sites, become familiar with its history.

**2. Even though English is widely spoken in Rouen, French is the predominant language there. However, knowing a few fundamental French expressions can significantly improve your communication and demonstrate respect for the local way of life.

**3. The Euro (€) is the currency in use in Rouen. For modest transactions, make sure you have some local currency available because not all locations could take credit cards, particularly in more traditional communities.

**4. Food: Rouen's rich agricultural heritage is reflected in its diverse food scene. Enjoy regional favorites like seafood platters, apple-based cuisine, and Camembert cheese. Don't pass up the opportunity to discover regional markets and bakeries for genuine delicacies.

**5. Layers and weather-appropriate apparel should be brought because of the temperate maritime climate. For touring the city's picturesque streets and cobblestone pathways, it's imperative to wear comfortable walking shoes.

**6. Rouen is easily reachable from Paris and other adjacent cities because of its good train and road connections. Walking is the best form of transportation within the city's historic district due to its small size.

**7. Local Protocol: The French appreciate politeness and respect. When dining and talking with locals, be courteous and say "Bonjour" (french for "good day") and "Merci" (thank you) to them.

**8. Rouen is home to a variety of museums and attractions, including the Gros Horloge and the Musée des Beaux-Arts. To make the most of your time, find out the opening times and any entrance requirements before your visit.

**9. Cultural Sensitivity: Be cognizant of the historical and cultural importance of locations like the Rouen

Cathedral and those connected to Joan of Arc. When you go there, be sensitive and respectful.

10. Market Days: Explore local culture by shopping in Rouen's markets, where you may buy local crafts, fresh foods, and one-of-a-kind trinkets. To prepare for your visit, do some market research ahead of time.

2. Organizing Your Travel

2.1 The Ideal Time to vVsit Rouen:

Planning a pleasant trip to this charming city requires selecting the ideal time to visit Rouen. The best time to visit mostly depends on your choices and the activities you hope to partake in, as each season offers a distinctive experience.

It's a pleasure to travel to Rouen in the **spring (March to May)** when the city comes alive with blossoming flowers and comfortable weather. Compared to the busiest travel period, the streets are less congested, allowing for a more leisurely exploration of the city's highlights. The delightful coolness of the day makes it perfect for sightseeing walks and excursions to outdoor locations like the gardens surrounding the Rouen Cathedral.

Summer (June to August): With its pleasant, bright weather, Rouen is a popular destination throughout the summer. With various festivals, outdoor activities, and bustling markets, this is the city's liveliest time. Though there may be more people at attractions and lodgings due to the increased tourist activities. This could be the best time to visit if you like the energy of summer festivals and don't mind the crowds.

Autumn (September to November): The fall is a wonderful season to visit Rouen as the summer throng starts to thin out and the city develops a tranquil atmosphere. You can engage in outdoor activities like strolling along the Seine River and visiting local markets because the weather is still pretty moderate. A touch of color is added to the environment by the fall foliage, making for stunning panoramas throughout the city.

Winter in Rouen is marked by colder temperatures and a calmer atmosphere (December to February). While some sites may only be open for a portion of the year, the city's historic beauty is still evident. The chance to discover Rouen's cultural and historical landmarks away from the masses is only available during the winter. The festive markets and decorations that the holiday season provides also give the city's streets a magical feel.

2.2 Visa and Entry Requirements:

Understanding the visa and entry procedures is an essential first step for anyone organizing a trip to Rouen to guarantee a simple and trouble-free journey. Here are some general recommendations on visas and entry into France for the majority of international travelers as of my most recent knowledge update in September 2021:

-**Visa Requirements:** Many nationals, notably those of the United States, Canada, and the European Union, are exempt from needing visas for brief stays in France (up to 90 days). This is often regarded as falling under the Schengen Agreement, which permits visa-free travel between some European nations.

-**Passport Validity:** The validity of your passport must extend at least three months past the day you want to depart France. Always verify the validity of your passport long before your intended departure date.

-**Stay Length**: Visitors without a visa may remain in France for up to 90 days within 180 days. You might need to apply for a different kind of visa if you intend to stay longer or have special travel objectives (such as a job, education, or long-term residence).

-**Proof of Funds:** Some passengers could be asked to provide documentation proving they have the money to support their stay in France.

-Return/Onward Ticket: You may be required to show documentation of a return or onward ticket from France to prove your intention to depart the country within the allotted term.

-**Entry Requirements:** You can be asked for details about your trip when you arrive in France, such as why you're there and where you plan to stay. Be ready to respond to inquiries from immigration authorities.

Please be aware that visa and entry requirements sometimes vary, so you must make sure you have the most recent information by contacting the French embassy or consulate in your country before you travel.

2.3 Travel Insurance

Travel insurance is a crucial but frequently underestimated component of travel preparation that can offer priceless security and peace of mind during your trip to Rouen. Having the proper travel insurance can protect you from unforeseen difficulties when you're taking a stroll along the Seine River, taking in the city's gastronomic delights, or touring its historical monuments.

-**Medical Coverage:** Travel insurance often pays for medical costs, which can be quite important if you get sick or hurt while traveling. It may cover hospital stays, doctor visits, and transportation for urgent medical needs.

-Trip Cancellation/Interruption: Because life may be unpredictable, plans may occasionally need to be modified. If your trip is cut short or canceled due to unforeseen occurrences like illness, personal emergencies, or other covered situations, travel insurance may be able to pay you for non-refundable charges.

-Lost Baggage and Personal Effects: Travel insurance will help you replace lost or stolen luggage and lessen the inconvenience if your luggage is delayed, misplaced, or stolen while you are traveling.

-Travel Delay: Travel insurance can reimburse you for additional costs paid as a result of a delay in your travel arrangements caused by events beyond your control (such as weather-related interruptions).

-Emergency support: Access to emergency support services, such as language challenges, medical referrals, and travel-related counseling, is frequently included with travel insurance.

Review the policy conditions, coverage limits, and any exclusions thoroughly before acquiring travel insurance. To select insurance that meets your demands, think about your unique travel tastes and needs. Although it comes at an additional expense, travel insurance can provide priceless security and help make sure that your trip to Rouen is remembered for all the right reasons.

2.4 What to Pack for a Trip to Rouen

It's important to take your time while packing for your vacation to Rouen to make sure you're ready for the variety of activities, climate, and cultural experiences the city has to offer. Here is a thorough list of what to bring to make the most of your trip:

-** **Pack a variety of clothes** because Rouen's weather might change throughout the year. For spring and summer, pack a few light layers, such as a light jacket, a pair of comfortable walking shoes, and breathable clothing. Pack thicker layers, a waterproof jacket, and warm accessories like scarves and gloves for the fall and winter.

-**Adaptor and Chargers:** Be sure to bring the correct power adaptor for your electrical equipment, as France utilizes European plugs. Chargers for your phone, camera, and other electronics should be packed.

-**Travel Documents:** Maintain orderly organization of all your necessary travel documents in a safe pouch. This contains your passport, visa (if necessary), information about your trip insurance, hotel reservations, tickets for your flights, and any pertinent contact information.

-**Medicines and Toiletries:** Bring any prescription drugs you may need, along with a simple first-aid kit. Don't forget personal hygiene products, hand sanitizer, sunscreen, and insect repellent.

-**Electronics**: Think about taking a portable power bank for your devices in addition to chargers. A tiny flashlight is useful for nighttime exploration.

-A comfy daypack is necessary for transporting your necessities while visiting the city. Pick one with secured compartments and zippers to protect your stuff.

-**Trip Guidebook or App:** While having access to digital resources is practical, having a physical trip guidebook or a dependable travel app can offer insightful information, maps, and suggestions even without an internet connection.

-**Reusable Water Bottle**: It's important to drink enough water while exploring. Bring a reusable water bottle with you so you may fill it up as needed.

- Carry some **local cash (Euros)** with you for little transactions, fares on public transit, and locations where credit cards might not be accepted.

- **Camera and Accessories:** Use a camera and any necessary extras, like memory cards, extra batteries, and a camera bag for protection, to document your time in Rouen.

-**Umbrella**: Given the sporadic rain, owning a tiny, portable umbrella can come in handy during unexpected downpours.

-**Sunglasses and Hat:** During the warmer months, shield your eyes from the sun's rays with sunglasses and a wide-brimmed hat.

-**Walking Shoes**:** For touring Rouen's cobblestone streets and historical buildings, you must have a pair of comfortable walking shoes. To avoid pain, make sure your shoes are broken in before your journey.

- Foldable, reusable bags are useful for transporting groceries, souvenirs, and unforeseen purchases.

-**Adaptive attire:** As a gesture of respect, carry modest attire that covers your shoulders and knees if you intend to visit religious sites.

You can guarantee you have everything you need for a relaxing and delightful trip to Rouen by packing thoughtfully. To make the most of your trip, adjust your packing list to the weather, your scheduled activities, and your tastes.

2.5 Language and Communication

Understanding communication and linguistic dynamics can substantially improve your travel experience, so keep this in mind as you plan your trip to Rouen. What you need to know is as follows:

-**Language:** Rouen speaks French, which is the official language of France. Even while many locals, particularly in tourist locations, may speak some English, making an effort to speak a few simple French words can go a long way in promoting favorable encounters.

-**Navigation**: Knowing a little bit of French can come in handy when figuring out how to use public transportation, read signs, and ask for directions. Learn the prevalent terminology used in the industries of transportation, dining, and attractions.

-**Translation Apps**: To overcome linguistic barriers, download translation software for your smartphone. You can use these apps to translate text, and speech, and even get helpful phrases for certain circumstances.

-**Cultural Sensitivity:** Being aware of French traditions and manners can make it easier for you to handle social settings. Using "Bonjour" (good day), "S'il vous plaît" (please), and "Merci" (thank you) might help you build a respectful rapport with locals.

- **Tourist Information:** Rouen's top attractions frequently provide information in English and other languages. To make sure you don't forget anything, it's a good idea to learn about the attractions and gather information before your visit.

-**Navigating Menus:** Eating out is an essential component of every trip. If you're not familiar with the phrases used in French cuisine, translation software or a small translation book in your pocket will help you understand menus and place orders with confidence.

2.6 Currency and Financial Issues

A pleasant journey to Rouen depends on having a solid understanding of money matters and the currency. What you need to know is as follows:

-**The Euro (€) is** France's official unit of exchange. For modest purchases, particularly in markets and local businesses, it is wise to have some cash in euros on hand.

-**ATMs:** ATMs, often referred to as "distributeurs automatiques de billets" (DABs), are extensively available in Rouen and accept the majority of popular credit and debit cards. Be mindful of any overseas transaction fees your bank may impose on card or ATM withdrawals.

-Currency Exchange: Airports, banks, and exchange bureaus all offer currency exchange services. Although these services are practical, they could have greater costs and worse exchange rates than ATMs.

-Credit Cards: The majority of hotels, restaurants, stores, and tourist sites accept major credit and debit cards including Visa and MasterCard. For smaller businesses that might not accept cards, it's wise to have some cash on hand.

- Tipping is normally included in the bill in France, however, leaving a modest tip (between 5 and 10 percent) is appreciated for good service. If a service fee has already been added, check the bill.

2.7 Travel Budget

For your trip to Rouen, creating a travel budget is essential to making the most of your vacation without going over budget. The split of potential costs to think about is as follows:

-**Accommodation:** Research your lodging options and allot money for motels, dorms, or rental homes. Prices can change depending on the area, quality, and season.

-**Transportation:** Set aside money for local transportation inside the city as well as travel by plane or train to and from Rouen. For convenience, think about getting a transportation pass.

-**Meals: Consider** the price of meals, snacks, and beverages. Although dining in cafés and restaurants in Rouen is a lovely experience, it's important to plan for these costs.

-**Activities and Attractions:** Entrance fees apply to several of Rouen's attractions. To include cultural activities, guided tours, and museums in your budget, do some research on their expenses.

-**Souvenirs and Shopping:** Allocate a percentage of your spending plan for shopping, whether it's for trinkets, regional crafts, or one-of-a-kind finds from marketplaces.

-**Miscellaneous Expenses:** Include unanticipated costs like gratuities, last-minute purchases, and surcharges.

-**Travel Insurance:** Don't overlook budgeting for the price of travel insurance. Although it adds to the cost, it offers vital protection and assurance.

-**Currency Conversion:** When using your credit or debit card for purchases, be mindful of exchange rates and any conversion costs.

-**Emergency Fund:** Having a reserve fund is advisable in case of unforeseen costs or crises.

You can allocate money wisely and make wise judgments about your spending during your trip to

Rouen by preparing and researching your trip in advance. By doing this, you can have a fulfilling time while remaining within your means.

3. Rouen's Transportation

3.1 How to Get to Rouen

By train, bus, and airplane, Rouen is well connected to other significant French and European cities.

1. By train: Rouen's primary train station is called Gare de Rouen. It is situated in the city's core and is accessible via both regional trains and TGV trains, which travel at high speeds. To major cities including Paris, London, Brussels, and others, there are direct train connections.

2. By bus: Several bus companies offer transportation to Rouen from other French and European towns. The Gare Routière de Rouen is Rouen's primary bus terminal. Various bus companies serve it, including Flixbus, Eurolines, and Ouibus, and it is close to the train station.

3. By air: The Rouen-Normandie Airport, which is roughly 15 kilometers from the city center, serves Rouen. From several French towns, including Paris,

Lyon, and Marseille, there are direct flights to Rouen. A few international flights are also available, notably ones to London and Brussels.

3.2 Rouen's public Transit

The TCAR (Transports en Commun de l'Agglomération Rouennaise) manages the city of Rouen's public transportation system. A subway, bus, and tram network are all run by TCAR.

1. Metro: Rouen's metro system consists of two lines, Line 1 and Line 2. Line 1 and Line 2 both travel from the city's center to the city's north and south, respectively. Train frequency fluctuates throughout the day based on the time of day on the metro, which operates from 5:30 am to 12:30 am.

2. Bus: The bus system in Rouen consists of more than 50 lines. According to the line, the frequency of the buses ranges from 5:30 am to 12:30 am.

3. Tram: Rouen's tram system consists of four lines. The trams run from 5:30 am to 12:30 am, with different lines having different tram frequencies.

The TCAR also runs the Noctambus night bus service. The Noctambus has three lines that span the city's center and the neighboring districts, and it operates from 12:30 am to 5:30 am.

At metro stations, bus stops, and the TCAR customer service center, tickets for the TCAR can be purchased at ticket machines. Online ticket sales are also available.

A single ticket is available for €1.60. Additionally, daily, weekly, and monthly tickets are offered.

3.3 Rouen Automobile Rental

Both at the airport and in the city center of Rouen, there are numerous automobile rental agencies in operation. Some of the more well-liked choices are as follows:

1. Avis: Avis has offices in Rouen and is a well-known international vehicle rental firm. You can reserve a car in person or online.

2. Another well-known worldwide vehicle rental company with offices in Rouen is Budget. You can reserve a car in person or online.

3. Sixt: Sixt is a high-end automobile rental agency with Rouen locations. You can reserve a car in person or online.

4. A significant vehicle rental company with offices in Rouen is Europcar. You can reserve a car in person or online.

5. Enterprise: With operations in Rouen, Enterprise is a low-cost vehicle rental agency. You can reserve a car in person or online.

There are a few things to consider when hiring a car in Rouen:

I In France, 18 years of age is required to rent a car.

II. A valid driver's license and credit card in your name is required.

III. The cost of renting a car in Rouen varies based on the kind of vehicle, the season, and the length of the rental.

IV. When you reserve your rental car in advance, you typically receive a better bargain.

3.4 Rouen's taxi and ride-hailing services

In Rouen, you can also use taxis and ride-hailing services. Some of the more well-liked choices are as follows:

1. Taxis: Although they might be pricey, taxis are a dependable way to move around Rouen. Starting at €2.60, the fee increases by €1.10 each kilometer.

2. Uber is a well-known ride-hailing service that is accessible in Rouen. The prices are typically less expensive than cabs, however, there may not always be a choice.

3. Bolt: Bolt is another well-known ride-hailing option in Rouen. The prices are comparable to Uber.

Before beginning your journey, it's crucial to agree on the fee while using a taxi or ride-hailing service in Rouen. Additionally, confirm the taxi or ride-hailing service has a license.

4. Accommodation

4.1 Luxurious Accommodations & Historic Hotels in Rouen

There are numerous luxury hotels and historic hotels in the city of Rouen, which has a rich history and culture. The top choices are as follows:

1. Hotel de Bourgtheroulde: This five-star establishment is set in a lovely mansion from the fifteenth century. There is a Michelin-starred restaurant, a rooftop terrace with amazing city views, and a spa.

2. Le Clos des Remparts: This four-star hotel is housed in a convent from the 17th century. It offers a tranquil garden, a pool, and a bar with live entertainment.

3. Hotel Le Charme Normand: This three-star establishment is housed in a lovely 19th-century

structure. It boasts a welcoming bar and a restaurant that serves typical Norman fare.

4. Located in the city's center and adjacent to the cathedral and museums is the 4-star Hotel des Arts. Views of the Seine River may be seen from the rooftop patio.

5. Hotel le Nouveau Monde: Housed in a 19th-century structure, this hotel has four stars. There is a spa, a gym, and a piano bar there.

These are just a few of Rouen's many excellent historic and luxury hotels. Think about your preferences, your spending limit, and the hotel's location while selecting a place to stay.

4.2 Charming Guesthouses and Small B&Bs in Rouen

Rouen also features a lot of small B&Bs and attractive guesthouses if you're seeking a more private and charming lodging alternative. The top choices are as follows:

1. La Maison d': This B&B is housed in a stunning townhouse from the 17th century. There are just 4 rooms total, and each has a distinct personality.

2. Le Petit Trianon: This inn is situated in a serene residential neighborhood. It comprises 5 rooms, each of which is decorated in a classic French manner.

3. La Cour des Loges: This inn is housed in a structure that dates back to the sixteenth century. There are six rooms total, each with a separate terrace.

4. L'Escale Normande: This bed and breakfast is housed in a former barn. It contains four rustically designed rooms.

5. Le Hameau des Artistes: This inn is situated in an old artists' settlement. It features five rooms, each of which is furnished differently.

These are only a handful of the fantastic little B&Bs and lovely guesthouses in Rouen. Consider your budget, your hobbies, and the location of the lodging when selecting a B&B or guesthouse.

4.3 Economical Accommodations in Rouen

In Rouen, there are still many excellent lodging options if you're on a tight budget. Here are some suggestions:

1. Hostels: Several hostels in Rouen provide both private rooms and dorm beds. A fantastic way to meet other travelers and save money on lodging is by staying in a hostel.

2. Airbnb: A fantastic resource for finding inexpensive lodging in Rouen is Airbnb. Apartments, rooms, and even complete homes can be rented from local hosts.

3. Camping: There are several campgrounds close to Rouen that provide inexpensive lodging and access to outdoor pursuits.

4. Shared apartments: Shared apartments in Rouen are advertised on several websites. This is a fantastic way to meet new people and save money on lodging.

5. Homestays are an excellent way to learn about French culture and save money on lodging. You'll stay with a local family and eat meals prepared at home.

Take your requirements and tastes into account while selecting a Rouen lodging option that is inexpensive. A hostel or Airbnb is an excellent choice if you are traveling in a group. A shared apartment or homestay are fantastic options if you want a more private experience.

4.4 Vacation Rental in Rouen

You can also rent a holiday home in Rouen if you're seeking a more roomy and autonomous lodging choice.

Apartments, homes, and villas are all possible vacation rentals. Compared to hotels or B&Bs, they provide more room and solitude.

The following elements should be taken into account while picking a Rouen holiday rental:

1. The number of bedrooms and bathrooms: If you are traveling in a group, you will require a rental with adequate bedrooms and bathrooms.

2. Location: Take into account where the rental is about the places you want to go.

3. Amenities: Some rental homes provide extras like a kitchen, a pool, or a washer and dryer.

4. Price: The cost of vacation rentals can range from affordable to opulent.

5. Discovering Rouen

There are numerous ancient districts to discover in Rouen, a city with a rich history and culture. Here are some of the top ones:

5.1 Historic Districts

The Rouen Cathedral, the Gros-Horloge, and the Joan of Arc Memorial are among the city's most well-known attractions, and the Old Town (Vieux Rouen) is where the majority of them are located.

1. The Old Town is a fantastic location for exploring the shops, cafes, tiny alleys, and passageways while taking in the ambiance.

2. Quartier Saint-Marc: This quaint neighborhood is just south of the Old Town and is distinguished by its classic Norman homes.

The Saint-Marc Church, a stunning specimen of Gothic architecture, is another building in the neighborhood.

3. Located to the east of the Old Town, the Quartier Saint-Nicaise is renowned for its bustling atmosphere.

The area is an excellent place to go out on the town because it has so many bars, eateries, and cafes.

4. Quartier des Antiquaires: To the north of the Old Town, this area is well-known for its antique stores.

5.2 Rouen Cathedral

In the center of Rouen sits the stunning Gothic cathedral known as the Rouen Cathedral. It is a UNESCO World Heritage Site and one of the most well-known cathedrals in all of France.

500 years were spent, beginning in the 12th century, constructing the cathedral. Its exquisite carvings and

stained glass windows make it a masterwork of Gothic architecture.

The public is welcome to take tours of the cathedral. A general tour, a tour of the towers, and a visit to the treasury are just a few of the numerous tours that are offered.

5.2.1 Tours of Cathedrals

The nave, the choir, and the stained glass windows are all included in the basic tour of the cathedral, which lasts about an hour.

You can climb to the top of the buildings during the 30-minute tower tour for breathtaking city views.

You may see the cathedral's collection of sacred treasures, including gold and silver objects, jewels, and vestments, during the 20-minute treasury tour.

5.2.2 Light Display

Every evening, there is a light show at the Rouen Cathedral. The light display narrates the cathedral's architectural and historical development.

The light show is a breathtaking and powerful event that shouldn't be missed. It's a wonderful opportunity to get a fresh perspective of the cathedral.

Here are some pointers for visiting the cathedral in Rouen:

1.* Purchase your tickets in advance, particularly if you are going during a popular time of year.

2. * Because you'll be walking a lot, wear comfortable shoes.

3. * Give yourself plenty of time to visit the cathedral and admire its splendor.

4. * Reserve your tickets in advance if you're thinking about going on a tour.

5. * The light display is a well-attended event; get there early to secure a decent location.

5.3 Joan of Arc memorials

The city of Rouen, where Joan of Arc was burned at the stake in 1431, honors her as a national hero of France. In Rouen, there are several Joan of Arc memorials worth visiting:

5.3.1 The Joan of Arc Museum

The Archbishop's Palace, where Joan of Arc was questioned and tried, is home to the Joan of Arc Museum. The museum chronicles Joan of Arc's life and contributions.

The museum features a collection of memorabilia from Joan of Arc, such as her clothing, helmet, and sword.

The tale of her life is also told in a multimedia exhibit at the museum.

5.3.2 Place du Vieux-Marché

Joan of Arc was executed at the stake in the Place du Vieux-Marché. With a statue of Joan of Arc, the square is now a serene park.

The statue, which was built in 1896, is a well-liked tourist attraction. The square serves as a memorial to Joan of Arc's tragic death.

5.3.3 Saint Joan of Arc Church

The Place du Vieux-Marché is close to the Church of Saint Joan of Arc. The church, which honors Joan of Arc, was constructed in the first decades of the 20th century.

A stunning stained glass window in the chapel features a picture of Joan of Arc. Fans of Joan of Arc frequently make pilgrimages to the church.

5.4 Museum of Fine Arts

In Rouen, France, there is a museum of fine arts called the Musée des Beaux-Arts. It is one of the most significant museums in France and has about 100,000 pieces of art, including decorative arts, sculptures, paintings, and drawings.

The museum was established in 1801 and is located in a stunning structure created by Louis Sauvageot. The museum's collection spans several historical eras and artistic movements, from the Middle Ages to the present.

The following are some of the highlights of the museum's collection:

1. The museum's collection of paintings includes works by some of the world's finest artists, including Rubens, Rembrandt, Velázquez, and Van Gogh.

2. Rodin, Maillol, and Carpeaux are just a few of the French and European sculptors whose works may be found in the museum.

3. Drawings by some of the greatest draughtsmen in history, including Leonardo da Vinci, Michelangelo, and Raphael, are on display at the museum.

4. The museum offers a collection of decorative arts, which includes china, tapestries, and furniture.

Anyone interested in art ought to visit the Musée des Beaux-Arts. The museum's hours are 10:00 am–6:00 pm, and adults must pay €12 to enter.

5.5 Rouen's Botanical Garden

In the French city of Rouen, there is a public garden called the Botanical Garden. It was established in 1635 and is one of France's oldest botanical gardens.

There are many different kinds of flora living in the 8-hectare garden, including trees, flowers, and bushes. In addition, the garden features a library, a museum, and a greenhouse.

The Botanical Garden of Rouen is a well-liked tourist spot and a wonderful place to unwind and take in the scenery. The garden is free to enter and is open from 7:30 am to 7:30 pm.

The Botanical Garden of Rouen's features include the following:

1 . The greenhouse is where a variety of tropical plants, including orchids, cacti, and succulents, may be found.

2. There is a collection of books and manuscripts on botany at the library.

3. The museum contains a selection of exhibits on the development of botany.

4. More than 1,000 roses can be seen in the rose garden.

5. The Japanese garden was created with inspiration from traditional Japanese gardens.

5.6 Rouen's Modern Architecture

The city of Rouen has a long history and a vibrant culture, but it is now embracing modern architecture. In Rouen, several contemporary structures are interesting to view, including:

5.6.1 Kindarena

In Rouen, there is a sporting facility called the Kindarena. It was constructed in 2012 and serves as the Rouen Métropole Basket team's home arena.

A stunning structure with a wave-like roof is the Kindarena. It is a well-liked tourist attraction and is built of glass and steel.

5.6.2 Panorama XXL

In Rouen, there is a 360-degree panoramic museum called the Panorama XXL. It debuted in 2017 and provides breathtaking city views.

The Panorama XXL has a massive screen that is 100 meters in diameter and is built in former grain storage. The museum features displays about Rouen's and the surrounding area's history.

5.6.3 Flaubert Bridge

The Flaubert Bridge is a Rouen pedestrian and bicycle bridge. After the French author Gustave Flaubert, it debuted in 2008.

A remarkable bridge with a curved form is the Flaubert Bridge. It is constructed of steel and glass and is a well-liked location for photographs.

5.7 Rouen Parks & Gardens

There are many lovely parks and gardens to visit in the green spaces that make up Rouen. Here are some of the top ones:

5.7.1 Jardin des Plantes

In the center of Rouen is a botanical garden called Jardin des Plantes. It was established in 1635 and is one of France's oldest botanical gardens.

There are many different kinds of flora living in the 8-hectare garden, including trees, flowers, and bushes. In addition, the garden features a library, a museum, and a greenhouse.

A well-liked tourist spot and a wonderful place to unwind and take in the outdoors is the Jardin des Plantes. The garden is free to enter and is open from 7:30 am to 7:30 pm.

Here are some of the Jardin des Plantes' highlights:

1. The greenhouse is where a variety of tropical plants, including orchids, cacti, and succulents, may be found.

2. There is a collection of books and manuscripts on botany at the library.

3. The museum contains a selection of exhibits on the development of botany.

4. More than 1,000 roses can be seen in the rose garden.

5. The Japanese garden was created with inspiration from traditional Japanese gardens.

Spending the afternoon at the Jardin des Plantes is lovely and relaxing. It is an excellent location for learning about botany as well as for unwinding and taking in the outdoors.

5.7.2 Square Verdrel

In the heart of Rouen, there is a little park called The Square Verdrel. Both locals and tourists like visiting it.

A fountain, a statue of Joan of Arc, and a variety of trees and flowers can be found in the park. A fantastic area to unwind and observe people is The Square Verdrel.

5.7.3 Parc Grammont

North of Rouen, there is a sizable park called Parc Grammont. Both joggers and families frequent the area.

In addition to a lake, a playground, and a skate park, the park is also home to a variety of trees and flowers. It's a terrific idea to get some exercise and enjoy the outdoors at the Parc Grammont.

6. Galleries and Museums

6.1 The Museum of Antiquities

In Rouen, France, there is a museum called the Musée des Antiquités. It is devoted to Normandy's history, from the Stone Age through the Middle Ages. The museum, which is situated in a medieval abbey, was established in 1831.

Over 100,000 items, including paintings, sculptures, and artifacts from antiquity, are housed in the museum's collection. Paleolithic, Neolithic, Bronze Age, Iron Age, Roman, and Gallo-Roman artifacts are included in the collection.

The following are some of the highlights of the museum's collection:

1.* A selection of tools and weaponry from the Paleolithic era

2. * A mosaic from the Roman era

3. * A group of historical sculptures

4. * A work by French painter Nicolas Poussin

A remarkable museum that gives an insight into Normandy's past is the Musée des Antiquités. Anyone interested in archaeology or French history ought to go there.

6.2 Museum of the History of Medicine

In Rouen, France, there is a museum called the Musée Flaubert et d'Histoire de la Médecine. It is devoted to the history of medicine as well as the life and writings of the French author Gustave Flaubert. The museum, based in the former Hôtel-Dieu de Rouen, a former hospital, was established in 1907.

Over 20,000 items, including manuscripts, books, paintings, sculptures, and medical equipment, can be found in the museum's collection. Novel drafts by

Flaubert are included in the collection, along with other items important to his life and work.

The following are some of the highlights of the museum's collection:

1. A copy of Madame Bovary by Gustave Flaubert
2. A selection of 18th- and 19th-century medical equipment
3. A work by French painter Eugène Delacroix

A remarkable museum that provides insights into Gustave Flaubert's life and work as well as the history of medicine is the Musée Flaubert et d'Histoire de la Médecine.

6.3 Museum of Ceramics

In Rouen, France, there is a museum called the Musée de la Céramique. Its focus is on the background of ceramics. The museum, which is situated in a medieval abbey, was established in 1827.

The museum features a collection of nearly 20,000 items dating from the fourth century BC to the present, including ceramics from all around the world. Ceramics from China, Japan, Greece, Rome, Italy, France, Spain, and Portugal are included in the collection.

The following are some of the highlights of the museum's collection:

1. A fourth-century BC Chinese vase
2. A seventeenth-century Japanese tea set
3. A vase made in Greece around the fifth century BC
4. A Roman amphora dating back to the first century AD

A wonderful museum that provides a look into the history of ceramics from all around the world is the Musée de la Céramique. Anyone interested in ceramics or the history of art must go there.

6.4 Musée des Beaux-Arts

In Rouen, France, there is a museum of fine arts called the Musée des Beaux-Arts. It is one of the most significant museums in France and has about 100,000 pieces of art, including decorative arts, sculptures, paintings, and drawings.

The museum was established in 1801 and is located in a stunning structure created by Louis Sauvageot. The museum's collection spans several historical eras and artistic movements, from the Middle Ages to the present.

The following are some of the highlights of the museum's collection:

1. Works of art by some of history's finest painters, including Rubens, Rembrandt, Velázquez, and Van Gogh.

2. Sculptures created by French and European artists like Carpeaux, Maillol, and Rodin.

3. Drawings by some of the world's finest draughtsmen, including Raphael, Michelangelo, and Leonardo da Vinci.

4. Decorative arts, such as ceramics, tapestries, and furniture.

Anyone interested in art ought to visit the Musée des Beaux-Arts. The museum's hours are 10:00 am–6:00 pm, and adults must pay €12 to enter.

6.5 Le Secq des Tournelles Museum

France's Rouen is home to the musée Le Secq des Tournelles. Its focus is on decorative arts, particularly ironwork. Alexandre Le Secq des Tournelles founded it in 1889.

The museum is located in a stunning old 18th-century mansion. Its collection totals about 20,000 items, including ceramics, ironwork, furniture, and tapestries.

The world's most significant collection of ironwork is located here. It has items from the Middle Ages to the current day that are from throughout Europe. A collection of Japanese prints and sketches is also housed in the museum.

Anyone interested in decorative arts must visit the musée Le Secq des Tournelles. The museum's hours are 10:00 am–6:00 pm, and adults must pay €8 to enter.

6.6 Pierre Corneille Museum

In Rouen, France, there is a museum called the Musée Pierre Corneille. It is devoted to the dramatist Pierre Corneille's life and achievements. The Société des Amis de Pierre Corneille created it in 1914.

A house from the 17th century that belonged to Pierre Corneille now serves as the museum's home. Over 2000 items are in its collection, including manuscripts, books, paintings, sculptures, and possessions of Corneille.

The world's most significant manuscript collection is located there. It contains drafts of Corneille's plays, poetry, and letters. It also contains drafts of his plays.

For those who are interested in French literature, a trip to the Musée Pierre Corneille is a must. The museum's hours are 10:00 am–6:00 pm, and adults can enter for €7.

These are only a few of Rouen's numerous museums and galleries. If you

7. Cultural Celebrations and Events

7.1 Festival of Joan of Arc

The Joan of Arc Festival is an annual celebration honoring Joan of Arc's life and contributions that takes place in Rouen, France. A variety of events, including historical reenactments, plays, concerts, and fireworks, are presented during the festival, which takes place in late May or early June.

Since the festival's debut in 1920, it has become more and more well-known. Over 200,000 people attended the festival in 2019.

The historical reenactment of Joan of Arc's trial and execution is the festival's high point. The reenactment takes place in the Place du Vieux-Marché, the site of Joan of Arc's 1431 stake burning.

The festival also includes several additional activities, such as:

1. Plays about the legacy and life of Joan of Arc. Play about Joan of Arc's life and legacy
2. Concerts including Renaissance and medieval music
3. Displays of fireworks
4. Food and beverage booths

The Joan of Arc Festival is a fantastic way to find out more about the life and contributions of one of France's most well-known historical heroes. It is also a wonderful chance to learn about Rouen's culture and history.

7.2 Festival of the Orchestras Cavaillé-Coll

An annual organ festival takes place in Rouen, France, under the name Festival des Orgues Cavaillé-Coll. The Cavaillé-Coll organs are used for a variety of concerts that are presented as part of the festival, which takes place in late September or early October.

French organ maker Aristide Cavaillé-Coll was born in 1811 and died in 1899. His instruments can be found in many of the most well-known churches and performance venues in the entire world. He is regarded as one of the best organ builders of all time.

It's a wonderful opportunity to hear some of the greatest organists in the world perform on some of the world's finest organs at the Festival des Orgues Cavaillé-Coll. A wide range of educational programs, including lectures and workshops, are also included in the festival.

7.3 Normandie Impressionniste Festival

The annual Normandy Impressionist Festival is held in the French region of Normandy. The festival, which takes place in late July or early August, includes a range of Impressionism-related activities, such as art exhibitions, concerts, and walking tours.

The event honors the rich cultural tradition of the region, which is recognized as the cradle of impressionism in

Normandy. The festival offers a range of activities, such as:

1. Impressionist painting exhibitions
2. Classical music performances that are influenced by Impressionism
3. Walking excursions to sites of Impressionism
4. Wine and food pairings

7.4 Rouen Christmas Market

Every year, the French city of Rouen hosts the Rouen Christmas Market. The market, which sells Christmas-themed foods, beverages, and presents, is held from late November through December.

The market is situated in the same location where Joan of Arc was burned at the stake in 1431, the Place du Vieux-Marché. The market draws more than 2 million tourists a year to its major tourist attractions.

There are more than 200 booths in the market selling a range of Christmas items, such as:

1. Holiday trees
2. Nativity displays
3. Holiday decorations
4. Holiday fare and beverages
5. Holiday presents

The market also hosts several events, such as:

1. Concerts for Christmas
2. Holiday light displays
3. Workshops for Christmas

The Rouen Christmas Market is a wonderful location to take in the wonder of French Christmas. It has a joyful and enchanted ambiance that is sure to make you feel festive.

7.5 International Film Festival in Rouen

An annual film festival takes place in Rouen, France, called the Rouen International Film Festival. The festival presents a selection of movies from all over the world and is held in late October or early November.

Since its founding in 1979, the festival has become more and more well-known. Over 100,000 people attended the festival in 2019.

The festival presents a range of movies, such as:

1. Feature movies
2. Short movies
3. Documentary films
4. Independent movies

The festival also offers a range of activities, such as:

1. Interviews with directors
2. Seminars
3. Events

7.6 Rouen Geek Festival

An annual celebration called the Rouen Geek Festival takes place in Rouen, France. The festival, which takes place in late September or early October, includes a range of geek culture-related activities, such as those focused on video games, comics, anime, and science fiction.

The festival offers a range of activities, such as:

1. Video game competitions
2. Signings of comic books
3. Anime movie showings
4. Panels for science fiction
5. Cosplay competitions

The Rouen Geek Festival is a fantastic opportunity to celebrate geek culture and connect with like-minded individuals. It's a fantastic chance to discover new comic books, science fiction, anime, and video games.

7.7 Rouen Comedy Festival

An annual event is held in Rouen, France, called the Rouen Comedy Event. The festival, which takes place in late February or early March, offers a selection of stand-up comedy performances by both regional and worldwide comics.

The festival presents a range of performances, including:

1. Live comedy performances
2. Open-mic events
3. Seminars

7.8 Festival of Nations in Rouen

An annual celebration called the Rouen Festival of Nations takes place in Rouen, France. The festival, which incorporates a range of activities honoring many cultures from around the world, is held annually in late July or early August.

The festival offers a range of activities, such as:

1.* Food vendors
2. * Performances of music
3. * Performances of dance
4. * Cultural displays
5. * Classical games

A fantastic approach to discovering the diversity of the world and learning about various cultures is to attend the Rouen Festival of Nations. It is a fantastic chance to socialize and have fun as well.

8. Regional Food and Dining

8.1 Traditional Norman Dishes

France's Normandy is a region renowned for its extensive gastronomic heritage. The region's cuisine is influenced by both its agricultural produce and proximity to the sea.

Some of the most well-liked traditional Norman dishes are listed below:

1. Tripe, onions, carrots, and white wine are all ingredients in the stew known as "Tripes à la mode de Caen." The meal is typically served with a side of potatoes and is substantial.

2. A sausage called **Andouillette de Vire** is created from chitterlings, pork, and seasonings. It is a dish with a strong flavor that is frequently served with mustard.

3. The tiny pancakes known as "crêpes" can be stuffed with a variety of savory or sweet toppings. In Normandy, they are a well-liked dessert or snack.

4. Small pastries called *Mignardises* are frequently offered as a dessert or an after-dinner treat. They are available in a range of tastes, including fruit, chocolate, and vanilla.

5. Apple brandy called **Calvados** is made in Normandy. It is frequently consumed straight or added to drinks.

8.2 Gastronomic Dining Establishments

Several gastronomy restaurants in Rouen provide traditional Norman fare. Here are some of the top ones:

1. Le Champ des Possibles, a Michelin-starred establishment, serves a tasting menu of contemporary French cuisine that emphasizes regional ingredients.

2.   La Couronne is a long-standing Norman establishment that dates back more than 200 years. It is renowned for its traditional fare, including andouillette de Vire and stripes prepared in the style of Caen.

3. The bistro **Le Bistrot des Gourmets** provides a more relaxed dining environment. It is renowned for its hearty cuisine, including crêpes and kig ha farz, a Breton specialty cooked with lamb, sausage, and buckwheat.

4.   La Table d'Élise is a wine bar with a small menu of traditional French fare. It's a terrific spot for a leisurely meal and to sample regional wines.

5.   Le Comptoir Normand is a restaurant with a market theme that serves a selection of meals produced with local, seasonal products. It's a fantastic location to sample some Normandy cuisine.

8.3 Patisseries and Bakeries

Numerous bakeries and patisseries in Rouen sell a range of sweet and savory pastries. Here are some of the top ones:

1. Au Petit Rouennais is a well-known French bakery that has been operating for more than a century. It is renowned for its croissants, macarons, and mille-feuilles.

2. A bakery that specializes in sourdough bread is called **La Maison du Pain**. Quiches and tarts are among the numerous pastries that are available.

3. "Les Délices Normands" is a patisserie that specializes in Norman desserts like "kouign-amann" and "galette des rois."

4. A crêperie that serves a selection of savory galettes is called **La Crêperie des Arts**.

5. Le Comptoir Gourmand is a bakery with a market feel that serves a selection of pastries made with seasonal, fresh ingredients.

8.4 Local Markets and Food Tours

There are several regional markets in Rouen where you may buy fresh, in-season produce, meats, cheeses, and other regional goods. Here are some of the top ones:

1. The traditional market **Marché aux Herbes** is held every day but Sunday. It is in the center of the city and a fantastic location for buying products like fresh food and flowers.

2. Every Saturday morning, there is a food market called Marché Saint-Marc. It is a fantastic location to find regional produce, meats, cheeses, and other food goods and is close to the Rouen Cathedral.

3. Every Sunday morning, an antique market called Marché des Antiquaires is conducted. It is a terrific spot to find antiques, collectibles, and other unique stuff and is close to the spot du Vieux-Marché.

8.5 Calvados and Cider Tastings

Numerous locations in Rouen provide samples of the cider and calvados that are famous throughout Normandy. Here are some of the top ones:

1. A range of calvados tastings are available at the museum and tasting room known as **La Maison du Calvados**.

2. A sample of cider and calvados is available at the organic farm **La Ferme du Bec Hellouin**.

3. Le Comptoir Normand is a restaurant with a market theme that serves a selection of calvados and ciders.

9. Recommended Restaurants

9.1 Gill

Featuring a tasting menu of modern French cuisine with a focus on regional ingredients, Gill is a Michelin-starred establishment. Maxime Mulot, the chef, is renowned for his imaginative and creative meals, which are prepared using the finest seasonal ingredients.

The seasonal tasting menu features delicacies like roasted pigeon with celeriac and foie gras and seared scallops with cauliflower purée and truffles. The service is flawless, and the wine list is very great.

Although Gill is quite pricey, it is worthwhile for a special event. The restaurant's cozy and exquisite dining area is housed in a stunning old townhouse in the center of Rouen.

9.2 La Couronne

La Couronne is a long-running, conventional Norman restaurant that dates back more than 200 years. It is renowned for its traditional fare, including andouillette de Vire and tripes prepared in the style of Caen.

The dining area is furnished with exposed beams and stone walls, and the restaurant is housed in a historic building in the center of Rouen. The pricing is fair, and the service is courteous and attentive.

Traditional Norman cuisine can be enjoyed at La Couronne. The atmosphere is genuine, and the cuisine is filling and excellent.

9.3 La Pêcherie

In Rouen's Old Town, there is a seafood restaurant called La Pêcherie. The restaurant offers a wonderful view of the Seine River and a selection of meals made with fresh seafood, including fish soup, moules frites, and grilled oysters.

The costs are fair, and the service is courteous and effective. La Pêcherie is a fantastic location to eat delectable seafood while admiring the Seine River.

They sample the following dishes at these restaurants:

1. At Gill, you should try the roasted pigeon with celeriac and foie gras as well as the seared scallops with cauliflower purée and truffles.

2. Try the tripes à la mode de Caen or the andouillette de Vire at La Couronne.

3. You can sample grilled oysters, moules frites, or fish soup at La Pêcherie.

9.4 Le Champlain

Overview:
A tasting menu of modern French cuisine with a focus on regional ingredients is available at the

Michelin-starred restaurant Le Champlain. Maxime Mulot, the chef, is renowned for his imaginative and creative meals, which are prepared using the finest seasonal ingredients.

* The tasting menu changes seasonally, but you can anticipate finding dishes like roasted pigeon with celeriac and foie gras or seared scallops with cauliflower purée and truffles. The service is flawless, and the wine list is very great.

* Although Le Champlain is a tad pricey, it is well worth it for a special occasion. The restaurant's cozy and exquisite dining area is housed in a stunning old townhouse in the center of Rouen.

* **Menu**

* Le Champlain's tasting menu changes seasonally, but you can always count on finding inventive and imaginative items. The chef experiments freely and only

employs the freshest seasonal ingredients. You might find the following foods on the menu:

1. Seared scallops with truffles and cauliflower purée
2. Roasted pigeon served with foie gras and celeriac
3. Risotto with langoustine and black truffles
4. Roasted squab with black truffles and foie gras
5. Vanilla ice cream and chocolate soufflé
6. Wine

9.5 Le Bistrot des Artistes

Overview:

* The Old Town of Rouen is home to the classic French cafe Le Bistrot des Artistes. Crêpes and kig ha farz, a classic Breton meal prepared with lamb, sausage, and buckwheat, are two examples of the restaurant's home-style cooking.

* The dining area of the restaurant is furnished with exposed beams and stone walls, and it is housed in a wonderful old structure. The pricing is fair, and the service is courteous and attentive.

* Le Bistrot des Artistes is a fantastic location to enjoy traditional French food in a casual and welcoming atmosphere.

* **Menu**

Le Bistrot des Artistes' menu offers a selection of traditional French cuisine, including:
1. Crêpes
2. The Lorraine quiche
3. * Frites de steak
4. Kig ha farz.
5. Tartine tatin

10. Shopping and Souvenirs

10.1 Rue du Gros-Horloge (Pedestrian Street)

In Rouen's Old Town, there is a pedestrian street called Rue du Gros-Horloge. A wide range of establishments, including apparel stores, gift shops, and art galleries, are along this well-liked shopping boulevard.

The Gros-Horloge, a historic clock tower at the street's terminus, is the source of the street's name. One of Rouen's most recognizable sights and a well-liked tourist attraction is the clock tower.

The Rue du Gros-Horloge is a fantastic location to shop for Rouen-related gifts. Numerous stores are selling Norman specialties including calvados, gingerbread, and cider. Numerous more souvenirs are also available, including t-shirts, mugs, and magnets.

In addition to gift shops, apparel shops can be found on Rue du Gros-Horloge. You may choose from a range of designs and price points, so you're likely to find something you like. Additionally, there are a few art galleries on the street where you may look at some regional creations.

The Rue du Gros-Horloge is a fantastic location to go shopping in the afternoon. There is a lot to see and do on this busy boulevard.

10.2 Vieux-Marché Flea Market

The Old Town of Rouen hosts a weekly flea market called the Vieux-Marché. Antiques, treasures, and other unique stuff can be found there in abundance.

Every Sunday morning from 9 am until 6 pm, the market is open. The Place du Vieux-Marché, a sizable square in the center of the Old Town, is where it is situated.

The market is segmented into numerous areas, each of which focuses on a particular category of goods. There are categories for clothing, jewelry, home products, antiques, and collectibles. A space for food and beverages is also there.

The Vieux-Marché Flea Market has relatively affordable prices. On antiques and collectibles, you can get some fantastic prices. The market is a fantastic location to find one-of-a-kind presents and souvenirs.

A well-liked tourist destination is the Vieux-Marché Flea Market. It's a nice area to window shop and barter for a few hours. It is also a fantastic location to explore the native way of life.

10.3 Quaint Street (Rue Eau-de-Robec)

The Rouen neighborhood's Rue Eau-de-Robec is a charming boulevard dotted with individual stores and boutiques. Along with garments and accessories from regional designers, it is a terrific place to find one-of-a-kind presents and souvenirs.

The Robec River, which once ran through the area, inspired the street's name. The street's name hasn't changed even though the river was covered up in the 19th century.

The commercial district of Rue Eau-de-Robec is well-liked by both locals and visitors. It's a terrific area for exploring and shopping. Take your time and investigate; there are many hidden treasures to be discovered.

Traditional Norman goods including cider, calvados, and gingerbread are available in some of the stores on Rue Eau-de-Robec. Numerous more souvenirs are also available, including t-shirts, mugs, and magnets.

There are several apparel boutiques on Rue Eau-de-Robec in addition to souvenir shops. You may choose from a range of designs and price points, so you're likely to find something you like. Additionally, there are a few art galleries on the street where you may look at some regional creations.

The Rue Eau-de-Robec is a fantastic location to go shopping in the afternoon. There is a lot to see and do on this busy boulevard.

10.4 Boutiques and Designer Shops

Numerous designer shops and boutiques can be found in Rouen where fine apparel, accessories, and home products are sold. These shops can be found both in the heart of the city and in the neighborhood.

In Rouen, some of the most well-known stores are:

1. Les Petites Mains Normandes: This shop offers handcrafted ceramics, lace, and needlework as well as other traditional Norman goods.

2. Le Comptoir Normand: This shop offers a selection of Normandy-made goods, including food, wine, and trinkets.

3. La Maison du Cidre: This store offers Normandy-produced calvados and cider.

4. L'Atelier du Chocolat: This shop offers Normandy-made handcrafted chocolates.

5. La Cave du Patrimoine: This wine store offers wines from France's Normandy and other regions.

11. Day Trips From Rouen

11.1 Giverny and Monet's Gardens

A little village in Normandy called Giverny is well-known for its Claude Monet gardens. For more than 40 years, Monet lived and worked in Giverny, and his gardens are regarded as some of the most exquisite in the entire world.

The Impressionist Garden and the Water Garden are the two sections that make up the gardens. The flowers, trees, and bushes that Monet loved to paint are all present in the Impressionist Garden. A sizable pond and a Japanese bridge can be found in the Water Garden.

The gardens are a well-liked tourist site and are accessible to the general public. They are a fantastic site to spend a day taking in the splendor of nature and one of the most well-known painters' creations.

Giverny also contains a museum devoted to Monet's life and work in addition to the gardens. Along with Monet's paintings, the museum also has his personal effects and letters.

11.2 Honfleur and the Coast of Normandy

On the coast of Normandy, Honfleur is a lovely harbor city. It is a well-liked tourist site and is recognized for its fishing boats, colorful homes, and small alleyways.

Honfleur is a wonderful location to unwind and breathe in the coastal air. Fresh seafood and regional wines are available at several of the town's cafés and eateries.

Hikers and cyclists enjoy traveling to the Normandy coast as well. Numerous routes meander through the cliffs and woods.

Honfleur and the Normandy coast are excellent choices for day trips from Rouen if you're searching for something that combines history, culture, and gorgeous beauty.

11.3 Étretat and its Cliffs

A little town in Normandy called Étretat is well known for its white chalk cliffs. The cliffs abruptly rise from the water and reach heights of up to 150 meters.

The cliffs are a popular location for photographers and artists in Étretat, a well-known tourist destination. The cliffs may be reached by several hiking trails, and you can also take a boat ride to view them from the water.

Along with the cliffs, Étretat features a lovely beach and a quaint ancient town. The town has a lot of eateries and shops, making it a wonderful destination to spend the day exploring.

11.4 Château Gaillard in Les Andelys

The medieval castle Château Gaillard is located in the French town of Les Andelys in the Normandy region.

One of the most significant castles in Normandy, it was constructed in the 12th century by Richard the Lionheart. Château Gaillard in Les Andelys is shown in the picture.

On a cliff top overlooking the Seine River, the castle is situated. It is a huge building with towers and high walls. Since it was built to be impregnable, the fortress has never been taken by force.

Richard the Lionheart stayed at Château Gaillard while on the Third Crusade. The English and French used the fortress in the Hundred Years' War after he passed away. After some time, in the 16th century, it was abandoned.

Currently, Château Gaillard is a well-liked vacation spot. It is a well-kept castle and a fantastic location to study medieval military architecture.

11.5   Abbeys and Castles Nearby

In addition to Château Gaillard, the area around Rouen is home to a large number of other abbeys and castles. Here are some of the most well-liked:

1. The Abbey of Jumièges About 30 kilometers from Rouen, in the village of Jumièges, is where you'll find this abbey. It was one of the most significant abbeys in Normandy when it was founded in the seventh century. Despite being destroyed during the French Revolution, the abbey has since been renovated and is today a well-liked tourist attraction.

2. Château de Chenonceau: About 150 kilometers from Rouen, in the village of Chenonceaux, is where you'll find this castle. It was constructed in the 16th century and is among France's most stunning fortresses. A moat surrounds the castle, which also boasts a lovely garden.

3. The Palace of Versailles The town of Versailles, which is around 70 kilometers from Rouen, is where this castle is situated. It was constructed in the 17th century and served as the royal family of France's residence. One of the most well-liked tourist destinations in France, the castle is a UNESCO World Heritage Site.

4. The Abbey of Bec-Hellouin About 80 kilometers from Rouen, in the town of Bec-Hellouin, is where you'll find this abbey. It is one of the most significant abbeys in Normandy and was founded in the 11th century. The abbey is well known for its stunning architecture and its library, which houses a collection of old manuscripts.

5. The Castle of Gisors About 50 kilometers from Rouen, in the village of Gisors, is where you'll find this castle. It was one of the most significant castles in Normandy when it was erected in the 12th century. Despite being in ruins, the castle is a well-liked tourist attraction.

12. Nightlife in Rouen

12.1. Bars

The nightlife in Rouen is thriving and has plenty to offer everyone. Here are a few of the city's most well-liked bars:

1. *Le Tavern du Marché: This Old Town Tavern is a fantastic place to start your evening. There is a wide variety of beers and wines, and the environment is lively.

2. **Le Pub Irlandais" is an Irish bar in the Old Town that's a terrific place to catch a game or enjoy live music. It offers a wide variety of drinks and beers.

3. **Le Carré des Arts:** This bar is a terrific place to meet up with friends and is situated in the St. Marc neighborhood. It offers a wide variety of cocktails and a laid-back atmosphere.

4. **La Taverne Normande:** This Old Town pub is an excellent spot to sample regional cuisine and beverages. It has a warm and welcoming ambiance.

5. * **Le Speakeasy:** This Old Town bar is a terrific place to go out on the town. A good assortment of cocktails is available, and the setting is speakeasy-like.

12.2 Nightclubs in Rouen

Additionally, Rouen boasts a wide array of clubs that can accommodate different musical tastes. Here are a few of the city's most well-known clubs:

1. Le Cargo is a fun location to dance the night away and is located in the Old Town. Hip-hop and electronic music are both represented in a large variety.

2. Le Vauban, a club in the St. Marc neighborhood, is a terrific spot to catch live music. It can accommodate more than 1,000 people and is used for a range of events, including parties and concerts.

3. Le Chat Noir: This Old Town club is a terrific choice for a more laid-back evening out. It features a bar, and a dance floor, and frequently features live music.

4. The St. Marc neighborhood's La Machine du Moulin Rouge is a terrific venue to spend a night out with friends. It boasts a sizable dance floor and a range of music, from hip-hop to electronic.

5. Le Bureau This club, which is in Old Town, is a terrific choice if you want to have a more underground experience. It boasts a spooky, cozy ambiance and a wide variety of electronic music.

12.3 live Music Venues

The live music scene in Rouen is thriving, and there are several venues to select from. Here are some of the most well-liked:

1. Le Vauban, a club in the St. Marc neighborhood that features live music, is a terrific location to go. It can

accommodate more than 1,000 people and is used for a range of events, including parties and concerts.

2. Le 106: This Old Town location is a fantastic place to catch up-and-coming artists. It has a modest capacity and a laid-back vibe.

3. La Cartonnerie, a venue in the St. Marc neighborhood where you may catch more established musicians. It can accommodate more people and has a livelier atmosphere.

4. La Flèche d'Or is an excellent spot to view a range of music, from jazz to rock, and is located in the Old Town. It can accommodate a big crowd, too.

5. Le Café Charbon is a terrific place to view a more subterranean vibe. It is situated in the St. Marc neighborhood. It has a limited capacity and a cozy, dark interior.

12.4 Jazz bars in Rouen

There are several jazz bars in Rouen where you may have drinks and listen to live music. Here are some of the most well-liked:

1. Le Caveau des Ducs, for example, This Old Town Tavern is a fantastic location to enjoy traditional jazz. It has a modest capacity and a laid-back vibe.

2. Le Bilboquet: This St. Marc neighborhood bar is an excellent place to hear contemporary jazz. It can accommodate more people and has a livelier atmosphere.

3. The Jazz Club of Rouen This Old Town venue is a terrific place to catch up-and-coming jazz musicians performing. It has a tiny audience size and a loyal following.

4. La Javanaise This club, which is situated in the St. Marc neighborhood, offers a wide selection of jazz performances, from classic to contemporary. It can accommodate a big crowd, too.

Le Comptoir Normand: 5. This Old Town tavern is an excellent place to sample traditional Norman fare and beverages while enjoying jazz. It has a warm and welcoming ambiance.

13. Perfect 7 Days Itinerary

Day 1:

* One of France's most renowned Gothic cathedrals is the Notre-Dame Cathedral. The cathedral is a UNESCO World Heritage Site and is situated in the Old Town.

* Discover the Gros Horloge, a historic clock tower that serves as one of Rouen's emblems. A well-liked tourist attraction, the clock tower is situated in the Old Town.

* Explore the Old Town, a lovely neighborhood with winding streets and half-timbered homes. It's fun to roam around and discover the Old Town.

Day 2:

Visit the Joan of Arc Memorial, a memorial honoring the French heroine who perished at the hands of the English at Rouen in 1431. The memorial is a well-liked tourist attraction and is situated in Old Town.

* Visit the Museum of Fine Arts to view its collection of international paintings, sculptures, and other works of art. The Old Town Museum is a fantastic resource for learning about art history. Visit Rouen by boat and sail along the Seine River. The boat ride is a fantastic way to observe the city from a fresh angle and discover its past.

Day 3:

* Go to the Rouen Natural History Museum which has a collection of more than 2 million specimens of worldwide fauna, flora, and minerals. The museum, which is in the Old Town, is a fantastic site to learn about Normandy's natural heritage.

* Discover the stunning Gothic Saint-Maclou Church, which is situated in the Old Town. The church is renowned for its exquisite woodwork and stained glass windows.

Day 4:

* Go on a cruise down the Seine River, which runs through Rouen. The boat ride is a fantastic way to observe the city from a fresh angle and discover its past. Additionally, you can savor the stunning views of the surrounding countryside.

Day 5:

* Go trekking in the countryside of Normandy. There are numerous hiking trails available, varying in difficulty. Hiking trails can be found through fields, woodlands, and along the ocean.

Additional information about each activity is provided below:

1. Admission to the Natural History Museum of Rouen is €8 for adults and €5 for children, and it is open from 10 am to 6 pm.

2. The Saint-Maclou Church is free to enter and open from 9 am to 7 pm.

3. Several spots in Rouen offer boat tours on the Seine River. The cost varies according to how far you have to travel.

4. The Normandy landscape is home to a wide variety of hiking trails. Online or at the Rouen tourism office, you may discover information on the paths.

Day 6:
* Attend the **Rouen Comedy Festival**, which takes place in February each year. The event presents a range of international and French comedic performers.

* Alternately, go to the **Rouen International Film Festival**, which takes place in June each year. Feature films, documentaries, and short films from all around the world are presented during the festival.

Day 7:
* Savour Rouen's vibrant nightlife and local food. In Rouen, there are lots of fantastic restaurants that serve conventional Norman fare including seafood, calvados,

and cider. In the evening, have a night out in one of Rouen's numerous bars or clubs.

Additional information about each activity is provided below:

1. The Zénith de Rouen, a sizable music venue in the city, hosts the Rouen Comedy Festival. You can buy festival tickets at the box office or online.

2. Several locations in the city, including the Cinéma Le Jacques-Prévert and the Cinéma Le Gaumont, host the Rouen International Film Festival. You can buy festival tickets at the box office or online.

13 Useful Information

13.1 Tips for Health and Safety

1. Drink bottled water only since tap water might not be safe to consume.

2. Because the water in rivers and lakes could be contaminated, avoid swimming there.

3. Take precautions against pickpockets and pay attention to your surroundings.

4. Tell someone where you're going and when you anticipate returning if you're going on a hike in the country.

5. Be prepared for the heat by bringing a hat, sunglasses, and sunscreen.

6. Be mindful of the potential for food poisoning, particularly if you're eating street cuisine.

13.2 Local Customs and Etiquette

1. While French people are typically quite hospitable and friendly, it's vital to be aware of certain traditions and manners.

2. Even if you are only quickly meeting someone, it is considered courteous to shake their hand when you greet them.

3. Holding doors open for others and standing up when someone enters the room are further manners.

4. It is normal to give the waiter or waitress a modest tip (about 10%) when dining in a restaurant.

5. It is also regarded as polite to refrain from discussing religion or politics in casual conversation.

Printed in Great Britain
by Amazon

45812060R00066